BREACH

BRE

POEMS

NICOLE COOLEY

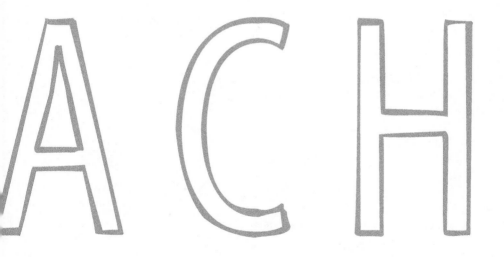

LOUISIANA STATE UNIVERSITY PRESS ⟩|⟨ BATON ROUGE

Published by Louisiana State University Press
Copyright © 2010 by Nicole Cooley
All rights reserved
Manufactured in the United States of America
LSU Press Paperback Original

DESIGNER: *Amanda McDonald Scallan*
TYPEFACES: *Whitman, text; Myriad, display*

Library of Congress Cataloging-in-Publication Data
Cooley, Nicole.
  Breach : poems / Nicole Cooley.
    p. cm.
  "LSU Press paperback original."
  ISBN 978-0-8071-3584-6 (pbk. : alk. paper)
  I. Title.
  PS3553.O5647B74 2010
  811'.54—dc22

                          2009022091

For my mother and my father
and all the people of the Gulf Coast

Here is your road, tying

you to its meanings: gorge, boulder, precipice.
Telescoped down, the hard and stone-green river
cutting fast and direct into the town.

—MURIEL RUKEYSER, "The Book of the Dead"

CONTENTS

ACKNOWLEDGMENTS

Some of these poems appeared, often in slightly different versions, in the following publications: "September Notebook," *Callaloo* 29:4 (2006), 1035–1037. © 2006 Charles H. Rowell. Reprinted with permission of The Johns Hopkins University Press; *Court Green:* "Write a Love Letter to Camellia Grill"; *Crab Orchard Review:* "Day of Commemoration"; *The Iowa Review:* "Dear City"; *Journal of Family Life:* "Monkey Hill"; *The Kenyon Review:* "Breach" and "I Spy a Hole, a Crack, a Leak"; *LIT:* "Piecework: Lower Ninth Ward"; *New England Review:* "Bayou La Batre, Alabama" and "Old Gulf Coast Postcards"; *Nimrod: An International Literary Journal:* "I'm Starting to Speak the Language"; *The Paterson Literary Review:* "Fieldwork"; *Ploughshares:* "Save Beach Elementary"; *Psychoanalytic Perspectives: A Journal of Integration and Innovation:* Excerpt from "Evacuation"; *Traffic:* "Tear Outs" and excerpt from "Evacuation"; *Weber: The Contemporary West:* "Biloxi Bay Bridge Still Out," "The House on Galvez Street," and "Self-Portrait: Concrete, Chalk, Floodwater;" "Debris" first appeared in *Women's Studies Quarterly* 36: 1& 2 (Spring/Summer 2008). All rights reserved. Reprinted with permission from The Feminist Press.

"Death of an American City" and "New Orleans Triptych," appeared in *Hurricane Blues: Poems about Katrina and Rita,* ed. Philip Kolin and Susan Swartout. Cape Girardeau: Southeast University Missouri State Press, 2006. "Topographies" was published as a limited-edition broadside by the Center for Book Arts, New York City, 2007.

My thanks to the Passaic Community College Poetry Center for recognizing "Fieldwork" as a 2007 Editor's Choice Award from the Allen Ginsberg Poetry Awards. Much gratitude to Queens College–The City University of New York for a sabbatical that enabled the writing of the book. Also I am grateful to the PSC–CUNY Award Program from the Research Foundation of the City University of New York. I am deeply thankful for the chance to work with LSU Press on this project and for the help of John Easterly and Neal Novak. Thank you to Chris Jordan for the cover photograph, which I have admired since I first saw it after the storm. Thanks to all who helped me: Nancy Austin, Pamela Barnett, Susan Bernofsky, Barbara Bowen, Nancy Comley, Peter Cooley, Jacki Cooley, Tonya Foster, Steve Gehrke, Amelie Hastie, Julia Johnson, Tim Liu, Cassandra Melendez, Nadine Meyer, Brad Richard, Talia Schaffer, Roger Sedarat, John Weir, Sally Wofford-Girand, and Elizabeth Zervigon. I am especially grateful to Kimiko Hahn and Julia Kasdorf. And to my sister Alissa Rowan, my brother Josh Cooley, and my daughters, Meridian and Arcadia, companions on the journey that led here. Most of all, I thank my husband, Alex Hinton, without whom I would never have written this book. Our dialogue about the world informs all my work, especially this one. Our love sustains me.

BREACH

Topographies

Marshy spillover is first to flood: where water
first met sand and pilings lost all anchor.

Where nothing rose above the surge, that wall
of black, black water. Where houses buckled, crumbled.

Where the storm's uneven scrawl erased.
While miles away I watched a map of TV weather,

the eyewall spinning closer. A coil of white, an X-ray.
I imagined my parents' house swept to its stone slab.

While I remembered sixth-grade science, how we traced the city
like a body, arterials draining in the wrong direction.

We shaded blue the channel called MR GO that pours
from the River to the Gulf, trench the storm water swallowed.

The levees overfilled, broke open. And I came home to see
the city grieving. The city drained then hacked apart.

i.

Breach

[Origin: bef 1000; ME *breche*, OE *broec* breaking]

Like a mouth packed shut, the levee wants to open *the act or a result of break-ing; break or rupture* it desires the water's fluorescence, the water's depth, the water's dirt *an infraction* and so the water, no pale lace collar fashioned of delicate mud, no mistress of careful spilling, the water in a storm surge cracks the floodwall apart *gap made in a wall, fortification, line of soldiers* sound of a gun shot and shot, sound of a bomb blast *a rift, a fissure, a severance of friendly relations* then silence as water erases, as water fills streets and takes everything with it: a hole of 200 feet *the breaking of waves, the dashing of surf* later you look on the city map *a violation, as of a law, trust, faith or promise* and it will be marked with a small red star like a bitter lipsticked kiss.

Levee, from the French *To Raise*

White families gather for a picnic, faces tilting into the sun,
on the bank of the river, on the crest of the levee.
Airplanes circle, movie cameras swing over the water.
To save New Orleans, we have to flood the rest.

On the bank of the river, on the crest of the levee,
we line up sticks of dynamite like toy soldiers. We will break it open.
To save New Orleans: we will flood the rest.
Flood the other parishes, flood St. Bernard, flood Plaquemines.

We line up sticks of dynamite. Soldiers will break it open,
this levee, the only cure for the swollen river,
that will flood St. Bernard, flood Plaquemines.
A shoulder of dirt, and, underneath, all hard blue clay,

this levee can cure the swollen river if we split it open.
We emptied St. Bernard, Plaquemines, Delacroix Island.
All your houses built on dirt, on hard blue clay,
will be destroyed to save the city, we explained.

We emptied St. Bernard, Plaquemines, Delacroix Island.
The white families open wicker picnic baskets.
Who will be destroyed? To save the city, we explained,
we ordered trucks to take you from your homes.

The white families open wicker baskets, set out their lunch.
They eat and wait to witness the explosion.
We ordered trucks to take people from their homes.
Now we begin. Watch the earth heave and settle.

We witness the explosion: dirt sputters into the sky.
The children cheer. Blast after blast after—
The earth heaves and settles. The flood begins.
The river swells and seeps from its banks.

We told you to evacuate. We had to break the levee.
Airplanes circle, movie cameras swing over the water.
To save the city, you had to leave. We told you.
White families gather for a picnic, faces tilting into the sun.

Evacuation

The vanishing is supposed to unfold steadily but it happens all at once—

1.
My mother says: We are not leaving. This is our home.

The morning of the hurricane, far from New Orleans, my daughter sits at our kitchen table with her crayons: "I'm drawing weather." She listens to my last phone conversation with my parents before the storm.

She outlines a dark green sun, sketches a cloud with the spokes of a wheel, turning, turning.

The morning of the hurricane, when I have quit yelling, begging, pleading with my parents to get out of the city, I tell my mother: Take the photo albums and leave them on a high shelf in the safest closet. One for me, Alissa, and Josh, of our childhoods.

To my father I ask: Do you have your poems?

2.
Click on *Report My Location*.
Hit *Click Here* to enter the name of the Missing Evacuee.

3.
The morning of the hurricane, the First-Ever-Mandatory-Evacuation-of-New-Orleans has been ordered by the mayor, and my parents pack a suitcase and take it to the house beside their church in the center of the city.

The church on Carrollton Avenue where, for years, my mother played the piano during evening service, where my brother was baptized, where my husband and I were married.

The church where they believe they will be safe.

4.

The morning of the hurricane, the sky in New York is a glare of bright, bright blue. The 9/11 sky, saturated, watercolored.

5.

Imagine myself in the church with them: stained-glass windows shattering, brick walls blown out, water filling pews, sliding over, up the steps to the altar.

Imagine myself boxed in the church Confessional: Yes, I was one of the unbelievers. I never worried about hurricanes during my own childhood, telling myself no Category Five ever hit the city when I lived there so it won't happen now.

6.

I'm sitting on the kitchen stairs hiding from my daughters, on the phone with my brother in Houston: *All roads to New Orleans are closed. The airport is submerged. Kenner is gone. East New Orleans is gone. Causeway Bridge is really messed up. I am worried about them but I don't know what to do.*

All the phones in New Orleans are down. All morning, I call my parents over and over.

Ring and ring and ring and ring—

7.
and nothing—

8.

It will be easier to imagine what will be lost if you keep it romantic: Live oaks in City Park. Japanese plums along St. Charles. The streetcar stumbling along its Uptown tracks as you rode home from school.

The oyster shells in the parking lot at the West End, how you kicked up crushed white dust with your sister. The rope swing at the river's edge. Riding your bike on the levee from Uptown over the Orleans Parish line.

It will be easier if you focus on location, if you empty the city's landscape.

If you don't remember your mother's insistence, *we are not leaving.*

9.
I tell my sister, we have to think rationally: we can call someone who will search the city to find them. She agrees. There are agencies to help: FEMA. The Red Cross. The Louisiana State Police.

10.
Ring and ring and ring and—

At my desk, I can only log-on for news—cnn.com (stream the video): *Watch the unanswered screams! Watch the rooftop rescues!*

11.
Imagine wind slamming the church house, water rising higher, higher, my father praying, my mother at the window reading The Book of Lamentations, copying the verses in her black and white notebook:

How the city sits solitary that was full of people!
She has become as a widow, who was great among the nations!
She who was a princess among the provinces is become tributary!

12.
I don't want my daughters to know about the hurricane, but they hear me whispering on the kitchen stairs, in three-way conversations with my sister and brother as we plan how to save my parents:

To my sister in St. Louis: Do you know if they took a radio?
To my brother in Houston: Do you think they know how to reach the roof?

My older daughter interrupts to ask me, what does *evacuate* mean?

13.
Four years before the storm, in New York, my husband and I watched the other disaster unfold on TV, as the sharp-edged burning drifted in our bedroom window, our daughter sleeping on my lap, too young to understand.

And we watched it and we swallowed the burning, we couldn't not breathe it in, but we were safe, the three of us, huddled together in our bed. None of us were missing.

14.
I copy lists, shelter numbers to call:

Orleans Parish, 504-565-7200
New Orleans Superdome.
Jefferson Parish, 504-349-5360
No shelters currently opened.
St. Bernard Parish, 504-278-4268
No shelters.

15.
On Tuesday, one day after the storm, we don't know where my parents are.

On the E train, traveling home under the East River, I imagine the subway tunnel cracking open, a sudden rushing of river water, all of us trapped. Water covering our seats, the yellow subway map, the poles we hold without thinking to keep from falling.

16.
FEMA. The Red Cross. The Louisiana State Police. I call and call and call. All the lines are busy.

17.
I can't reach my parents but the saturated watercolored run-down city is everywhere on TV. And on the news, I recognize what used to be Mid-City:

Downed oak trees along Carrollton, sandbags, roofing paper split, pile of black tiles on the neutral ground, branches torn and jumbled, power lines swinging like loose jump ropes,

Angelo Brocato's Bakery where my sister and I ate fluted paper cups of lemon ice, where our father took us after visits to the Art Museum, now barely visible behind twisted black fencing and a smashed-in unreadable sign.

18.
If the reported person has been located or you have updated information, please use the following Case ID to update the status of the missing/stranded person request you submitted to the Coast Guard. To make an update, go to "http://homeport.uscg.mil and: Enter the Case ID, select the "Safe/Located" checkbox if the reported person has been located, Case ID: Missing Person: Jacki Cooley

19.
My older daughter sits at the kitchen table drawing weather for her sister. "There is a hurricane in Arcadia's town so I'm making her a new house."

Beside her, my younger daughter watches the hurricane swirl on construction paper and helps her shade a roof's edge with her crayon, colors rising water red.

20.
The city is a bowl. The city is filling up. The breach in the 17th Street Canal is reported to be at least two blocks long.

The city is filling up, and it is the third day without word from my parents.

Picture family photo albums floating on the surface of the flood, pages swollen, loosening from their bindings: mother, father, sister, sister, brother.

21.
On the subway I make more lists that won't help anyone: *No Shelter. Shelter of Last Resort. Give me Shelter. Bob Dylan singing Shelter from the Storm.*

22.

When the storm ends, when the eye has passed over, when the sky above
New Orleans is clear again, the city's afterlife begins:

The city is a bowl, filled to the brim. A shaking, muddy surface, people
wading , boating, swimming through it to safety. The drainage pumps have
failed.

Picture my mother's silver mixing bowl floating out of her kitchen cupboard,
bowl full of dirt and bricks and wreckage.

Picture my mother praying at the window.

23.

On the third day, the waters are still rising, rising, rising.

24.

On the third day, my parents finally call and we find out they survived the storm.

Now you can leave, I tell them. Go to the Superdome. Find a way out of the city.
No, they tell me, the city outside the church is ruined: sheetrock split and broken
downed branches and tree trunks   floating cars   floating bodies no electricity   no clean
water

The city is locked down, my parents tell me, and no one can come in to the city and no
one can leave—

Therefore I am exercising my authority under the Louisiana Disaster Act and issuing a
Lock Out Order. We are at a catastrophic, disastrous impasse.

My happiness turns to a rising fury. There can be no evacuation. New Orleans is filled
and flooded and shut.

25.

A week after the hurricane, lying between my daughters in bed, a morning
rain lashing

against the windows,

a ribbon of silver-white water binding us to the house, the bedroom all
darkness,

and my body fills with relief—
a completely ordinary storm.

26.

On the subway I imagine: What if I were the one missing? Would my
daughters be frantic, looking?

27.

Trying to imagine my parents safe together, a water-tight world of two—

28.

At the park in New York, a child named Katrina wears pink cowboy boots,
rides the tire swing with my daughters.

I can't stop asking this girl to tell her name, just to hear the word over and
over again out loud.

Four Studies of the Afterlife

after Chris Jordan's photographs

Shower Stall and Remains of a Home with Levee in Background, Ninth Ward,
New Orleans

Don't you want to touch it? Like a surgeon reaching
a hand into a body, don't you want

to rummage here, run your fingers over the flat
pink tiles, still square, intact? Just as I tried

to climb inside the books my mother read to me,
to reassemble English countryside and wainscoted

baby nurseries on my bedroom floor. Don't you
feel drawn to sit on the edge of the cracked

bathtub, beside that window where the water
slammed the blind shut? To ruffle the

valence stuck on its rod? Watch the concrete
floodwall in the distance till your eyes burn and swarm and blur?

Tree Limbs in Lakeview Park, New Orleans

All in a tangle—
dendrites,
neurons,
a brain,
sliced and
scanned and ready
for dissection.
Or it's hair
gathered, snagged
from a brush
a mother dragged over

a crying child's
head.
Yes, someone forced
a hairball down that
throat.

Pants Rack in Women's Clothing Store, St. Bernard Parish

How you want it to tell a fortune!

Spin it like a sundial, this circular silver
rack still hung with clothes, with girls'
pants in ice cream colors:
mint, cool orange, teal. Pink flecked
with mold could almost shimmer.

How you want and want and want.
Like candy ruined in a box.

Remains of a Convenience Store, Slidell

Blackened, blackened glass bottles once thudded against
grass but now the grass is gone. All aluminum

cans as you can see will thin to rust under this
post-September light, this egg-yolk yellow rotting sun.

You and your mother drive and drive and she shows you
this Familiar, overturned. This Reversed.

This Inside Out. This Unfixed. After water
she explains, there is no water.

Do you want to hear it?

The landscape doused then ashed.

ii.

You, Author of Weather

stand outside the science center in a slur of rain

waiting for your mother, waiting to walk together to
the Exhibit of Cloud Rings where

your mother will push down the round metal plate to force
a stream of fog. This fog will ring and ring and spin

into a vortex—whirlpool, tornado, hurricane—or none
of these—

And the reader asks: Are you enjoying the Before?
When you're still allowed to create a storm—

When you bend down to swallow. A whole. A perfect
ring of cloud and it tastes like you

imagine sex will be because you're ten and
everything can be a metaphor and what you want

is to open your mouth to the hurricane's eye,
transparent and swirling and sweet.

Piecework Quilt, Lower Ninth Ward

And, behold, I, even I, do bring a flood of waters upon the earth, to destroy all flesh, wherein is the breath of life, from under heaven; and every thing that is in the earth shall die.

—GENESIS 6:17

First Square:
God created two of every, male and female. Two by two they were supposed to escape the flood. And the waters prevailed upon the earth—

Second Square:
From the shelter, Noah's wife had to imagine her bedroom window, the moon a cold disc floating.

Third Square:
Back on Delery Street, the sun glares on the dirt. The yard is flattened. The house is gone. She picks up pieces of a broken plate.

Fourth Square:
They went in two and two. Two of every. Or not. The ark rocking back and forth all night.

Fifth Square:
That August morning, after the storm, rain hung from the trees like hair. Then the water began to rise.

Sixth Square:
All the fountains of the great deep broken up. And the windows of heaven opened.

Seventh Square:
On the roof, the houses surrounded, the houses nearly disappeared, she waited for rescue.

Eighth Square:
The floodwall broke open, an explosion, a gun firing and firing up into the air.

Ninth Square:
After the storm, after the shelter, after she came back home—

Blank Square:

Vernacular

Wooden structures beyond saving—
Ride your bike to the streets of shotgun houses,
balloon frames set on stone, raised,
built to be safe from rising water.

Through the streets of shotgun houses, ride
to Mid-City. The Marigny. The Irish Channel.
Nothing in this city was safe from rising water.
Look for the waterline, faintest mark on wood.

Mid-City. The Marigny. The Irish Channel.
Twelve-foot floor-to-ceiling windows and no halls.
Look for the waterline, faintest mark on wood
that tells the story of the interior, the hidden ruin.

Twelve-foot floor-to-ceiling windows. No halls
connect the rooms that flow together. Nothing can tell
the interior's true story or the hidden ruin.
of this city unless you return to see it, unless

you connect the stories together. No one can tell:
the citizens are gone but the houses are a language.
Unless you return, you will not remember
the shotgun houses, how a gun fired in the front room

escapes out the back, how the citizens know a language
no one outside the city can speak.
How a gun shot through the front exits the back.
Each house a corridor of water. Outside no one

speaks this language or knows these neighborhoods,
block after block of balloon frames, raised.
Houses that filled and filled, in this city
believed to be beyond saving.

[handwritten annotations: letters A, B, C, D beside first stanza; "Story" with an X; "Repetition in form Mirrors Neighborhood" written vertically in left margin]

The Superdome: A Suite

after Spike Lee

Stage Set, Utah

At dawn the sky yawns white. She walks out of the new apartment
past shredded snow, lawns still flecked with ice, as if she could

walk to the end of winter. As if she could walk till she finds
the edge where one world becomes another, where she can see

the levee breach, where she steps out of this new life back into
the Flood-Swollen. Where she opens the door of her house

now stripped to its ribs. She could go back home if
she could turn the wall of black water into a sliding background, if

she could think of it all as a stage: her mother's blue willow
china smashed on concrete, the kitchen table splintered into sticks,

her children's school uniforms ripped and slick with mold and
all of it junked on the curb outside because the house is gone.

Auction Block

No, the sky shuts down in the story her grandmother has always told the
family, story of her own grandmother, story of being bought and sold, taken
from her children like a split tree limb, bought and sold and told her daughters
might be crying, crying for her but now forget them because they don't belong
to her.

Interview

Q: When you left the dome, how did you get up here?

A: On a bus that took us to the airport where we slept for three days. We were
told there would be buses to evacuate us in front of the Convention Center and

there weren't. Instead they drove us down Airline Highway and left us at the
door of baggage claim where they kept all the sick people, everyone waiting.

Q: Why didn't you evacuate when Mayor Nagin gave the order on Saturday?

Q: Why didn't you just leave?

Q: Why would you choose to be a refugee?

Shelter of Last Resort

No car, so after it happened, after the corner store man rowed me out
of the Ninth Ward in his boat, I walked there, over the bridge,

down Canal Street, to the only open shelter in the city, to the dome,
its white-mooned circle my girls had always called a UFO,

I thought of now as a place where I could go to be numb.
If I lived or died what did it matter when what I needed was to close up,

a flower's waxy petals rolling tight and shut forever.

Just the Beginning of the List of What She Lost

In her corner, on the green turf field, in her small space of no comfort, in
this theater of crying babies, sick people, of heat and the smell of everyone's
vinegared-sweat, in this land of no water but water everywhere outside she
listed, listed to stay awake, her body curled as small as she could make it—

One shotgun house, been in the family for three generations
one front room, three closets
a kitchen, walls once scattered with her own painted frieze of stars
a sideboard, a nightstand, a writing desk
a family album, fat and yellow-ribboned
full of school portraits of her daughters, year after year
and now—she imagines it—swollen with the damp, its spine broken

by water,
one family coming apart in pieces, sinking into the flood.

No Shelter

The water took her daughters.

The New Apartment

is too clean: in each corner wallboard meets wallboard, a perfect
flush seam over the carpet stretching like a sea of beige. And no toys,

no scattered pieces she yells at them to pick up: Connect Four or
Candyland or Chutes and Ladders. No Barbies, heads twisted off,

hair cut, faces scrawled with pen. Nothing here
but blonde-wood furniture, *generously donated by local people,*

the newspaper story said, *people who feel for the victims
of this disaster!* Nothing here but her and three empty dustless rooms.

Shelter

For those first two days, I got through

by remembering nothing,
by imagining instead
the slave auction, by thinking, *I've been here,* in another life,
by setting myself in that other story, in the body
of my great-great-grandmother,
by repeating:

Q: So what did you lose?
A: (unspoken) Everything.

The Painted Map of the United States

was where her daughters most liked to play, to jump from
state to school asphalt, from green to red, from Texas to
California, skip over their home state, the game was always not to

touch Louisiana. Back and forth they hopscotched till there was no
edge, no border between worlds, only that second of emptiness
beneath their feet, the moment they leave the ground.

Or now she knows there are only edges, there is nothing but
borders, only uncrossable divisions everywhere.

Tear Outs

Found poem, signs stuck in the dirt along Carrollton Avenue

Tree Service. Wood Preservation. Flood Car Repair.
Debris and Trash Removing.
Stump Removal. Tree Removal. Mold Removal.

Trailer Homes Delivered.
Demolition 4 Less. House Gutting.
Dear Santa, All We Want for Christmas is Gas.

New Orleans: One Block at a Time.

New Orleans Triptych

1.
On TV, the president stands in the dark city in his own private
circle of light, in a cornflower blue work shirt.

The president stands under klieg lights, in the shadow
of the statue of Andrew Jackson.

The president stands safely center stage.

>   Stage left: a women and her two children
>   who have climbed onto an attic roof
>   await rescue.

>   Stage right: with what has been described
>   as a loud cracking, as an explosion,
>   the breach occurs, over and over.

2.
How to read the breach. How to read an emptied city.

How to write the poem that reads the city,
that reveals

what's inside, a house to house search.
Spray painted: *an X means the house*
was empty. A number indicates how many

bodies were found.

On my desk miles away a snow globe of Jackson Square
I collected as a child—
now empty once was filled with water.

3.
At my kitchen table, my mother
draws a map of the breached levees

on my daughters' orange construction paper.
Daughters linked to that landscape who don't know it.

With a crayon my mother sketches the edge:

The Gulf. The Lake. East New Orleans. St. Bernard.
Here is the Ninth Ward. Here is Tremé. Here are

the canals where pumps were useless, the workers
already sent out of the city. Here is the river where

we live, where the levee didn't break.
At the kitchen table my daughters sit beside her,

listening. Houses marked X. The waterline

bisects each exterior but you can't
know what you'll find inside.

Come for a day, my mother tells me, *alone.*

This city is no place for children.

Burning/Missing/Flooded/Gone

Jackson Square in a box and empty.
Letters that spell *New Orleans* rubied.
Snow globe that fits inside your hand.

You're just a tourist watching
the invisible made visible on TV:
National Guard ready with loaded M-16s,

prepared to shoot the "looters."
Citizens who need water diapers food.
Shoot to kill, the president's orders.

East of the Quarter, a chemical fire burns.
Canals sandbagged with cement.
Your New Orleans ruined.

Bourbon Street is dry.
The Superdome fills with garbage
and families. *Shelter of Last Resort.*

Watch the story briefly on TV.
The commentator shakes her head.
Hard to believe this is the U.S.

It makes no difference.
Whose city is this? Not yours.
City of citizens who couldn't leave.

Jackson Square illuminated.
The president smiles, waves,
shuts off his stage light.

The world churns on. Forgets.
No snow globe of the Ninth Ward.
Or Gentilly. Or New Orleans East.

Citizens left on the I-10 bridge,
awaiting no rescue. Watch the surface
of the city tear like loose skin.

Dear City

For days the water holds on, will not release the city

*

and from up here I can't hold on to you, my city,

*

can't reach my parents who refused to leave the city.

*

In school we were taught: shaped like a bowl this city

*

can't withstand the weight of too much water, city

*

braced by dirt levees, all the floodwalls cracking. City

*

where I no longer live, where I am locked out, city

*

I lived in for so long, that has since lived in me, city

*

I must now watch on this computer screen, late-summer city—

*

"Watch the video of the worsening saturation of the city."

*

"Watch the video account of unanswered screams." City

*

fringed by a river, by a wide lake that spills over the city.

*

Oh, pale green city of my imagination. Now I can't carry you, city,

*

can't shutter you tight within my body to stop the repeating

*

of our jump-rope rhyme: Lost a city. Lost a city. Lost a city. Lost

epistrophe

Arabi

In other neighborhoods, houses stripped to beams and floorboards,
houses like sick fish, ready for gutting.

In other neighborhoods, trailers sit on cement blocks beside
houses crushed and flattened.

In other neighborhoods, Search and Rescue.

But here the landscape is fine grit and rubble,
the landscape is all flatness, the landscape is

                                        erased.

                        *

Now my father and I drive down St. Claude Avenue, not
talking—the view out the car window

evacuates speech. All we can do is look
at this place, where the morning of the hurricane

after hours of rain, the winds suddenly quieted,
where those who stayed stepped out on their porches,

walked into their yards, talked to neighbors across
the cyclone fence. Wondering how they avoided—

then turned and saw the first black wall of water
surge across the railroad tracks, saw it

wrench homes from their foundations, saw all
of St. Bernard Parish destroyed in fifteen minutes,

where those who stayed were lost in water poisoned
with spilled crude from Murphy Oil.

*

Across the city, that day, my parents waited
on the second floor of the brick house,

windows shuttered as if that gesture could protect.
Across the country, I willed them to break

through the ceiling to the attic, to wait on the roof for rescue.

*

The leaden water, the water lapping
at a roof like a lake's edge, the families stranded

on that roof, in that city, in that forgotten.
The families waiting,
the flatboat that never arrives.

Imagine the forgotten blackened with mold, water
turned into ash and cinder.

*

Now my father and I drive and drive and turn
looking for any intact

house, any car in a driveway, any
resident restaking a buckled fence

or piling bricks or raking debris
into garbage bags and there is nothing,

but street after street of lost front steps,
tar shingles, burned-off grass,

and I want to know who decides what is
unsavable and why were my parents

safe.

*

                    Here, for days, there was no

      salvage or searching for the dead or the living,
      and when finally the parish was sealed off,

      the survivors first housed in the jail, then waiting
      on Chalmette Slip, then crowded on a ferry for

      Algiers, all that was left were water moccasins
      twining through dead, salted grass, and still
                              no one came.

New Orleans East, A Cappella

Nothing here but trash, Italian for
like in the chapel and
he's set this for two or
more voices. Nothing but
what's left of his yard, pitched
front steps leading
to emptiness,
as the avenue's long
octaves end in dead
grass, scabbed yellow
and dry. A Second Line winds
down city streets
where no one lives.
Here's what he lost:
Set down the trumpet.
Shut the piano lid.
Muffle the drums.
This piece is scored
for the survivors. No
music but the voice could ever—
nothing accompanying.

Death of an American City, 2005

We are about to lose New Orleans.

Aerial view: too much swamp. Airport empty.

> *President Bush stood in Jackson Square and said, "There is no way to imagine America without New Orleans."*

Elysian Fields: a tangle of trees, cars covered in mud.

> *At this moment the reconstruction is a rudderless ship.*

Armstrong Park: grass gone, ground scabbed.

> *It all boils down to the levee system.*

St. Charles Avenue: streetcar gone, lampposts torn out by the roots.

> *People will clear garbage, live in tents*

Lower Ninth: houses marked in the search for bodies, an O, an X.

> *stalling till the next hurricane season*

Lakeview: Oriole Street, Lark Street: "We Tear Down Houses."

> *leaving nothing but a few shells for tourists to visit like a museum.*

Mid-City: street after street blue-roofed.

> *Total allocations for the wars in Iraq and Afghanistan and the war on terror have topped $300 billion.*

Aerial view: evacuation does not make vacant.

September Notebook

Like the magic porridge that takes
over the town, pours through the village,

fills, then empties, the streets—

—

It swallows everything in September and it happens twice

—

First, in New York the burning
seeped under our apartment door, into the window seams.

The sharp smell threaded through
my daughter's hair for days.
                              I pressed

my lips to her head.

—

Four years later in New Orleans
water surges over, under,
wrenches houses off stone foundations.
The floodwall cracks,
an explosion of gunfire.
Water surges around my parents' house.

—

I read that story to my daughter because

—

once upon a time there were two Septembers in two cities:
the one of the towers on fire
and the one of floodwaters rising

—

once upon a time my mother read it to me
when we leaned together in my canopy bed
when outside the window over the levee
the river was all flat green and quiet.

—

Now someone else is reading me the story. I crawl up
on her lap but she pushes me off and says:

Don't shut your eyes just because you can't watch
TV: the jumping couples from windows of Tower One,

the families, attics split open, in the Lower Nine, waiting for rescue.

—

Once upon a time it was the end of August and I
was on the phone with my parents, begging them to leave the city.

Fast forward to my parents' repeated answer:
                              this is our home.

I was telling my parents to go to the Superdome.

—

Today's American History Lesson, the voice says:
Once upon a time in 1927 white men blew up the Industrial Canal.

With a loud crack, they breached the levees.
They wanted to drive the black families out.

—

So when my daughter's class gathers at the flagpole for
a "patriotic song" "in commemoration" of "the event"—
the sky is a pure blue bowl
capable of holding nothing.

—

Here is the weather, the voice says, New York's bright sky in both Septembers.
Ever since, a clear early fall day is 9/11 weather.

—

I sit beside my mother on my bed.
I hold my daughter on my lap.

—

When the peasants run and the porridge blankets the streets
who will save them?

—

Today's History Lesson: It swallows and swallows and swallows.

—

I'd like to sit with her, Our Lady of the Breach.
Our Lady of the Burning City.
Our Lady of the Uncomforted.
I'd like to hold her hands down and whisper the lesson.

I'd like to force the floodwaters down her throat.

Debris

Wooden pilings from a shotgun house   pink insulation loose and threaded
a blonde-haired doll   a toilet   stucco crumbled to sand   a football helmet
the face of a metal fan   a sign: *Demolition Alert*   a mattress spiking metal   a
front door   a stove   a beach chair   a crushed pickup truck   a soup kettle
yellow bedsheet twisted in a tree   a rocking horse   a refrigerator with school
snapshots taped to the door   sandbags   a stop sign   a baby bottle   an armoire
shredded window screens   a sign: *Do Not Destroy*   dented fender of a school
bus   a leather couch   a claw-foot bathtub   a cyclone fence pleated like a fan
on poster board: *405 Paris Avenue*   a ketchup bottle   a wheelchair   a refrigera-
tor spray-painted *Help Me Jesus*   slab of wallboard spilled with mildew   door
like a blank eyehole   a sign: *For Sale by Owner*   a sign: *No Demo*   a sign: *Keep
Out*   a torn Blue Roof   unspooled yellow caution tape   sheetrock   black rot
a sign: *We're Coming Home*

Day of Commemoration

August 29, 2006

When I stand outside the Souvenir Mart on Canal Street, I can still smell
water through the cracked store front window.

When one year later mold's dull black edge could choke you.

When the woman from St. Bernard who sells T-shirts in the Quarter told me
she was evacuated to the parish prison.

When she says, "If we leave we take the city with us."

*

When the first pastor at the Convention Center Ceremony insists: the city
has a body.

When he stands before the blue serge curtain on stage and explains
the storm: a birth gone wrong.

When we now wait in the "Delivery Room of Opportunity" he says and
the audience says Amen, Amen.

When the storm was a cesarean birth, he says. The storm was a surgeon's
scalpel cutting open the city's body.

*

When we walk through the bright hot afternoon down Poydras to
the Superdome, shelter where I begged my parents to go.

When I walk behind The Black Men of Labor and Popular Ladies Social Aid
and Pleasure Club, behind the Tremé Brass Band.

When I finally understand

how little it matters—my lost childhood world—

—beside the Creole Wild West Mardi Gras Indians in feathers and sequins, beside the man who has wrapped his body in the flag to show New Orleans should not be forgotten.

Write a Love Note to Camellia Grill

Hundreds of post-it notes stuck on the windows—

Dear Camellia Grill, I can't bear the thought of you not being here. Dear
Streetcar, gone, that shuddered down the Avenue. Dear Neutral Ground,
    effaced.

*Last Meal at Camellia 18 days pre-K: potato, onion and cheese omelette,
pecan waffle, chocolate freeze.* Dear dead bleached grass. Dear leaf-

choked gutters. Dear Drainage Pumps. *Late night here drunk and LOVED it.*
Dear Levee. Dear Rusted Barge. Dear Rope Swing. *Your milkshakes bring all
    the boys.*

So many of us grew up eating here. We need you to open to feel more normal.
Dear Empty Grill. Dear Freeze Machine. Dear Jar of Marmalade. Dear Phone
    Book

split and open on a table. *My parents dated here and I dated here.*
Dear Chrome and Glass. Dear Counter, sparkled Linoleum. Dear Girl

I once was, smoking at that counter, writing boys names on a napkin.
New Orleans has lost Schwegmanns, K+B, McKenzies. It can't take another

New Orleans establishment to be gone forever. Dear Wind that Distills
the empty city. *I will come every day with 100 people.* Dear Damage.

I had my first date here. We got married. Come home! Dear Forgotten.
I'm going to stay hungry 4-ever. Dear Girl I once was. Dear Lost City.

Dear Girl Now Standing at the Window, reading: *I'm pregnant! Come back!*

At the Louisiana Children's Museum

for Meridian and Arcadia

Past the Cajun Cottage, the stunned tugboat
stuck in bright blue painted river water,
my daughters run to the craft room where they
will learn *New Orleans Architecture.*
Because Home is Where the Heart Is! Come and
Build a Home! Where I will sit beside them
at the table with no other children
building shotgun houses out of silver
tissue, wallpaper scraps. Where they will cut
out shutters, roofs and doors and glue each house
to a tongue depressor crayoned hot pink.
Where I will collect these houses to take
with me, as if I could save anything
from my city: roofs, shutters, doors, heavy
black waterline marking a porch, rusted
buckled fence, plywood sign strapped to a tree:
Please Respect Our Loss. Don't Enter.

I Spy a Hole, a Crack, a Leak

The water green gold, the pulse of water along his finger—

Once upon a time there was a daughter who insisted,
who brought her own two daughters back

to see the city. She couldn't leave them,
and so she drove them home while the toddler

screamed, "No New Orleans!" through Mississippi.
In that tale the daughter had read her daughters,

the boy, on his way to school, passes the dike,
sees the sea trickling in, tiny window of water.

In Slidell, the older girl tried to play I Spy With My Little Eye
but couldn't find any colors out the window.

The daughter, you see, wanted to teach a lesson
when she read that story. The Dutch Boy: how to avert disaster.

Perseverance. How a child could save a city!
She drove, over the Industrial Canal, through

the Ninth Ward out to St. Bernard. To Carrollton Avenue
past the park to Lakeview. Then Broadmoor

to South Galvez Street, to Story Street, to see
all the ruined houses she once lived in as a girl.

And while she drove the daughter drowned her daughters
out, found the crack in the landscape to slip through,

climbed inside her childhood dollhouse, roof sealed,
water rising up the tiny, narrow stairs, doll family

trapped in the attic, beating miniature fists on wood.

Bayou La Batre, Alabama

A small boat called *Nemesis* offers $5.00 tours
but the shrimpers are all stuck
in silt because the Corps won't touch them.

The boats are rusted, sails torn out,
boathouses a fringe of wood,
sign advertising *Crawfish* ripped by wind.

When we turn down Faith Street,
there is no one, only empty houses
scrawled with FEMA numbers, X or O.

More than half are gone:
families from Vietnam, Laos, Cambodia,
who worked the shrimp and oyster seasons.

Bayou Haircut is shut in the middle
of a salt-burned field where the Gulf
rose up to surge.

The High Tide Restaurant and Bakery
split into pieces of drywall, sheetrock,
roof smashed, windows shattered.

The late afternoon sky spreads its wings
behind the town, tints the landscape
silver, will not hold it.

There is no River of Heaven here,
nothing we imagine can save this place,
no one to ask what happened.

We walk to the Vietnamese Temple:
in a concrete garden Buddha waits, a Lotus
forever suspended, in the air, over his head,

Buddha dressed in saffron
beside a refrigerator duct-taped in the driveway,
each window of the empty holy place

cross-hatched with hurricane tape for the future.

Old Gulf Coast Postcards

Gulfport, Mississippi

Between the already-over and the now-gone, on a corner of the wrecked
downtown, in the Gulfport Pharmacy, my daughter and I spin the black
　　　rack—

Broadwater Beach. Biloxi Harbor. Pass Christian where two girls
splash in a Technicolor ocean so blue it burns your eyes.

Last year turned historical: *Welcome to Dauphin Island! Greetings
from Waveland!* Climb aboard the red and white ship

SS Hurricane Camille, docked at a wooden pier no longer outside.
At *The Real Southern Ante-Bellum House,* the azaleas

gleam play-doh pink, bunched and bursting off the columned porch.
We spin the rack, and I remember driving to Gulfport with my mother,

beaches my daughter will never see. Harbor, coast, skyline all relic.
Between the gone and the not-recovered, no one

steps out of their house to wave. No porch lights gleam.
Cadaver dogs sniff the dirt. At the edge of downtown, an ancient, twisted

oak lies uprooted, on its side, a sign labeling it *Alive.*

Fieldwork

Biloxi, Mississippi

On Beach Boulevard the sky hemorrhages light
over sugar-white sand, over the half-built casinos.

Imperial Palace. Treasure Bay. Over the half

of the highway from my window,
the half he sees from his. The Beau Rivage
will open on the first anniversary of the storm

while on the other side of 90,
the world is flattened to dirt and stippled grass.

The split landscape. The Gone and the Ready

to Save are there, but both are empty.
The Isle of Capri glitters in a sequin dress
and there are still no guests, the beach un-
peopled. We're taking notes.

As if details could save anyone who's left.
There's no one left

so we tell a story, one line at a time, we
imagine another couple:

In an atrium, in a cloud of giant butterflies
and golden mums as slot machines spit
coin after coin onto metal,
a woman lowers herself into three pools,
cold then warm then steaming, over and over again.

Her husband plays speed demon
all afternoon in the Category Five Arcade.

We'll let them meet later
on the 17th floor, in a heart-shaped bed.

She won't be the wife
on the other side of the highway,
sitting on the cracked slab scattered
with loose stones and mud.

But two sides of the highway do not equal speech.
Like the couple in the wedding chapel
under a garland of white Styrofoam,
we could suspend reality long enough to
stop looking, to turn to each other,

forgetting what's halved. What's whole.

Biloxi Bay Bridge Still Out

One year later, at the end of summer, light chopped into concrete blocks.
The bridge still out. From my truck I watch the highway grind to nothing.
The cars all have to turn back. I lean out my window and I tell them:
The eastern span was thrown fifty feet by wind.
At Beach Mini Mart, I wrote another message, spray-painted on plywood
over broken glass: *Good Buddy, Come Back.*
Parked at the edge of where the highway ends, I wait to tell them:
How water rose, receded, tumbled the girders, cracked the deck.
Now cars turn from the split asphalt, from the jumble of concrete pilings,
broken bridge spanning the unsaid.

Save Beach Elementary

Pascagoula, Mississippi

Do Not Enter the green stucco school,
cyclone fence studded
with debris and memorial wreaths,

monkey bars shadowing
blacktop where hopscotch, four square,
still scrawl yellow.

Do Not Touch the dodge ball
under the crepe myrtle tree or
the waterline ringing the building,

boarded windows eyes shut tight
against the flood. Do Not Destroy
this place the sign reads.

Late August, I'm walking
the streets in the Town
of No Children,

and it's true—I don't want
to imagine the children
who drowned here.

An X and an O blurred
in spray paint on a door don't
explain it

and past the recess yard,
along Market Street, sign after sign
stuck in the gutted,

on slabs of foundation,
in stacks of pilings
asking us to save the school.

And everywhere the voices—

Do Not Trespass   Do Not Demo   Do Not Come Here   Keep Out

Dauphin Island Field Notes

Dauphin Island, Alabama
   for Cassandra Melendez

1.

On the other side of the island, oil rigs once perched like flightless birds.
On the other side, houses are still painted mint green, soft butter yellow.
Houses stuck on crooked pilings, stilts collapsed like broken teeth.

I'm on my way back to the island where I once traveled,
on my twelfth grade field trip, I'm standing on the ferry, leaning
against the rail, not there yet but I remember

how I once easily erased this island, how I sat at my school desk
and with a pink diamond-shaped eraser rubbed
Dauphin Island out.

2.

                        How we were taught it was

Massacre Island in the days before New Orleans, before
Mobile. Capitol of the Louisiana Territory the island

was crowded with bones, stacks of cracked white piles of ash.
How The Army Corps of Engineers loaned our science class

the barracks for six days. Girls in hip boots we waded
out into the Gulf to fill pneumatic tubes with sediment to study

coastal erosion. How at night that coast was a necklace of lights.
Now sand has over-washed Bienville Boulevard. Now I want to turn back.

3.

Now there is more to copy, to write down. Now stand outside the Ship and
Shore and read the island's story on the bulletin board:

Yellow Hammer Building Systems: Modular Homes Certified for 140 mph winds

We can move your RV to Higher Ground! Before the hurricane comes call—

Attention, Katrina Victims. Your local volunteer organization has opened an office on Dauphin Island

Storm Protection Now! Free Estimates for hurricane shutters

For Sale: 1991 Chrysler New Yorker Blue No Storm Damage

4.
Damage Report

home name	condition
Foresight	destroyed
Voodoo Daddy	destroyed
Piping Plover	heavy damage, half of house gone

5.
I walk to the west end of the island where a narrow spit of land
dissolves, where our class spooned water to test sediment levels,
collected leaves in plastic specimen bags,

wrote up careful lists of the disappearing: sand shark,
spotted mackerel, on sheets of school loose leaf. The coast,
we learned, was eroding at a rate of five miles a year,

and we took in this information, we copied it down,
and we sat on the pier late at night and talked
about the future as if it would always include this coast

of scattered, sparkling lights.

6.
How easy it was, then, to smooth that page flat—

I'm Starting to Speak the Language

of disaster, he says, and we keep driving through Mississippi,
Highway 90, Hurricane Alley, on our way to New Orleans,
and he says, that one's blue-roofed, that one's gone,
and we stop to see an address on a tabletop leaned
against a tree, a number spray-painted on wood.
There's no house. *Private Property. Keep Out. Do Not Demo.*
We are here together on a tour of the Gone: three porch steps
For Sale By Owner, a beached trolley at the edge
of the road like a huge stunned animal—*Tour Historic Biloxi!*—
Gulfport Economy Inn. IHOP. Jefferson Davis's Beauvoir House.
All that's left of an address he calls *the new lexicon,*
the spray-painted X, the house marked O,
Dog Found. Stone foundation threaded with weeds
that are no language. Still, you can tell
where a house once stood, he says, by the clearing.
A front gate is *For Sale by Owner.* All that's left
of an address. Missing a whole story.

The House on Galvez Street

When we return from two weeks on the Gulf Coast, our house smells musty, damp, and I fill and set the soup pot on the burner, shake in oregano and red pepper, because I want to drown out any smell of water.

*

When my two-year-old sobs and kicks and screams on the kitchen floor I see her tantrum as a deep pool, murky and dark. I will myself to be calm, to float on the surface of the water.

*

When my mother tells me we lost boxes of family photographs in the flood of 1978, I remember how she couldn't bring me home from school because she was trapped in the house on South Galvez Street by the rising water.

*

When I drive over Canal to St. Claude Avenue, to the Ninth Ward, to Desire Street, the first shock is that the neighborhood looks burned and dried, each side street a parched throat, as if all the water has been washed away by water.

*

When we return from New Orleans, I can't shake the images from my head: flood-rusted, closed-down schools, trailers, empty because no one is given keys, house after house exposed and violated by water.

*

When the water first rose in our not-below-ground basement on Galvez Street, it reached the blue-roofed dollhouse my mother built, set on a low table, its cobblestone paper sidewalk she had made encircled by water.

*

When we return, I read *Alice in Wonderland* to my daughters but skip the white rabbit, skip the changing size, skip the magic bottle pleading Drink Me, turn only to the pool of tears, hold my daughters tightly in my lap, watch Alice drowning in her body's own water.

Disasterville

The Museum of Science and Industry,
Tampa, Florida

By legend hail is known as the white plague

and a hailstone sliced in half shows an onion's concentric rings,

reveals its travels from the top of the storm down.

I've skipped *Earthquakes* and *Wildfires*

to stay here, in *Storms*—

to spin the red and yellow Wheel of Misfortune

to predict the next Hundred Years Flood.

Beside the escalator a globe floats

on its stem, transparent bubble marked with women's names:

Ophelia, Katrina.

Please come to the next tornado show—2 minutes!

—

The *Hurricane Experience* plays over and over.

In a room before a floor-to-ceiling screen the movie of the storm surge,

the wall of rain, the wind, repeats.

You can stand before it for hours and it never
stops.

The video is stuck on endless repeat. Immersion theater lets weather enter

your body, lets wind turn into more than a soundtrack,

more than a dance beat pulsing

on a shiny floor.

—

It never stops. Only

at the exhibit of satellite radios

—*Disasters are capable of reducing*

humans to primitive survival mode. Voices carry

a few hundred feet—do I think of

my parents and their refusal and my own

yelling over the phone to force them

and my mother's voice: *This is our decision. We are not*

leaving. This is our home. Then I stand in the green glass

hurricane booth like a shower stall,

while a fan on the floor accelerates,

while a stream of wind burns my skin,

whips my hair into my mouth, slaps my sweater against my chest,

while a circle of teenagers watches, waiting

for their turn, and I stand

caught, suspended, caught.

Monkey Hill

for Elizabeth Zervigon

The best part was losing what we'd made, the moment when the rocket disappeared—

*

Lying beside my daughter in her bed all night, hand flat on her back, waiting for her skin to cool, twisting her wet hair away from her face. *Tell story,* she insists, *from when you were little.*

*

The story of twenty years later, when the river drowns, drowns, drowns the town?

*

In fifth grade science, we shot our rockets off the levee. Mrs. Cosgrove lined us up beside the hill, we lit each match, and each rocket, balsa wood and poster paint, arced over the flat water of the Mississippi, sank.

*

Welcome to New Orleans' oldest mountain!

*

No, not that story. Not yet—

"Cool sheet," I whisper, lifting it over my daughter's small hot body, as if I could erase her fever.

*

Fake hill, we all knew as kids, built by the city, built to show the children. A truckload of sand brought in and shoveled up in 1933.

*

Fourteen, I sat at the top and smoked my mother's cigarettes, watched the water, waited.
Already I called being ten *the past*. I could *look backward*.

*

We shot our rockets, our hands singed, ash on our palms.

*

Tell story, my daughter whispers, skin limned with sweat.

*

Fevered summer by the river: John Macalister, fifteen, drunk, swore he'd drive me to the top of the hill, up and over. *Easy,* he said, lifting my long hair off my neck as I leaned against him in his mother's station wagon.

*

River of dark rot beyond the hill. And what was under?

*

River of fever, fever of river, his hands in my hair, dirt and gravel sputtering under the wheels of the car.

His tongue tasted like metal sunk in mud.

*

No, Mrs. Cosgrove said, the city is not flat. It's below sea level. It's a bowl.

*

I picture the rockets drifting to the muddy river floor, lost ships in a bottle.

*

Tell the story:

when all the children of New Orleans have already left,
when I kick up loose gravel on the path back home.

Gone. And scatter. Scatter and scatter, gone—

Storyland

for Alissa

Covered in mud, cars are banked on the neutral ground
all the way out to City Park, where once my sister and I ran

through the Hickory Dickory Dock front gate,
crawled up the hot cement of Jack and Jill's Hill.

Swans peck at the edge of the canal, beside a FEMA trailer
turned into a hygiene station. No traffic lights glow along

Carrollton Avenue, but Snow White is still sleeping,
her face closed and peaceful just as it's been since 1956.

A Live Oak's limb fell on The Old Woman in a Shoe,
yet the fairy tale playground is intact, untouched and

surrounded by debris. How long can Pinocchio stand frozen
at the whale's mouth? How long can this city stay

two cities, one surviving and survived, one shadowed?
In Storyland, the fountains are dry, the Carousel still

shut down for repairs but the tilted funhouse is open.
Everything in the city has buckled, slipped, broken under

the weight of water. Everywhere a visitor could slide,
dizzy, back into childhood. Or board the Pirate Ship. Or

hide inside the Enchanted Castle. It was called
the unimaginable. Or it wasn't.

Divert the River

Undo the levees, unclasp the floodwall like a dress hooked tight

      at the neck.

          Send the river flooding wholesale

                into sediment-starved marshes,

downstream of New Orleans,

          to the bird-foot delta of the river's mouth.

Oh yes its mouth. See how it swallows, swallows and it chokes.

Listen, the bird-foot delta is an artifact

      of engineering so let's break it, let's wash it inland.

Rework sediment, carry it

          up the coast, its marshy bottom.

Then envision its future: a frail string

          of barrier islands will necklace the Louisiana coast.

Because every stream, storm drain and parking lot

          from the Rockies to the Appalachians drains into

the Mississippi river.

Our most navigable waterway. Sing to it. Listen. Take it apart.

Self-Portrait: Concrete, Chalk, Floodwater

I switch on the floodlight to rinse the front lawn clean.
Outside, with my daughter, I lie down on a river
of glittering asphalt, and she draws
my outline, carefully chalks my body
into our street. All summer there's been no rain,
the grass yellow and dry. I watch my girl

but look past her to see the other girl,
myself, on the levee, running over clean
cement, down to the water where rain's
blunt edge drums the mud of the river.
Then I imagine another street, a body
floating in the flood, family on a roof drawn

into the tightest circle. My daughter draws
around me, colors my absence, this girl
who once lived safely in my body.
What if all the houses on my street, their clean
blue shutters, bordered roses, were taken by the river,
wind slamming boards and shingles, rain

splitting roofs and fences, breaking steps, rain
swirling, lashing, ruining? My daughter draws
my hair, my arms, my face and there's no river
in this scene, just a mother and a girl,
and chalk that crumbles on the dry clean
grass like ash, like mold blackening the bodies

of the houses on my childhood street. A body
floats and sinks and no one claims it as rain
breaks open another house, buckles clean
wood, tears a door apart. Why am I always drawn
back to the other place, where a girl
stands at the levee's edge alone, where a river

flushes with light and promise, where that river
hasn't yet spilled over, flooding the body
of the city? I'd like to step outside myself, tell the girl
about the city's future, but endless, stumbling rain
would drown me out, eye of the storm drawing
always closer. Floodwater rinses nothing clean.

Nothing could keep any girl safe at the levee's edge.
Nothing I write could make a clean river of light.
Nothing will stop another storm erasing the city.

Disaster, A Poetics

after Jana Napoli's *Floodwall*

Like a coastline, the row of drawers is just potential emptiness, space of
rectangle after rectangle, space after bordered space.

Like that coastline's emptiness: the station where I now walk from the
E-train into the wide open, the World Trade Center, a cold wind blowing
through what's left of steel.

The station where I once waited to meet my husband, the afternoon
I found out I was pregnant.

*

Installed on the Liberty Street Bridge are the drawers the artist found
all that Fall in the yards and lawns of New Orleans.

To reach the exhibit, you walk along the green cyclone fence that hides
the excavation. Walk past the "viewing area" where a man sells
postcards of the towers.

Where is the viewing area for the hurricane?

*

That afternoon, five years ago, before the two Septembers, my husband rode
the escalator out of the PATH station. I stood at the top as he rose closer.
Inside my body the baby floated, untold, unknown, unfelt.

*

The drawers could have been found on the curb at my parents' house.

Drawers spread with pink-sprigged contact paper.
Drawers lined with official green felt.
Drawers folded tight with newsprint.

Drawers swollen so they'll never shut. But no one asks that of them now.

*

"The building at 130 Liberty Street, damaged on September 11, is being deconstructed."

*

610 drawers: How else could the artist document each lost household? How else to let debris reveal its narrative?

As if I am reading a line of text, I walk through the exhibit, right to left.

The drawers are syllables with too much space between them.

*

In the beginning, in that first September, posters and photographs filled fences and walls everywhere in the city. Now, *Post No Bills* the fence announces, fringed with torn newspaper and hand-lettered signs.

Now I walk out into the World Trade Center station where it is always winter—cold, subdued, stone-lit.

*

Meanwhile my parents' house still stands intact, in the ruined city, two blocks from the river.

Meanwhile I would like to go back and stand forever at the escalator, waiting for my husband, the baby spinning inside me, safe in the space of the not-yet.

*

Drawer of knives
sideboard drawer
junk drawer
drawer glued shut
nightstand drawer
secret hidden drawer

drawer fallen open
cash drawer
drawer folded with baby sleepers

*

Tell me why I always believed wrongly in loving the empty,
its stutter and thrum,

why all through childhood we walked on the levee and were never

afraid. Tell me how easy it is to love the vanishing when it stays a metaphor,
like the charms

baked in our wedding cake, each pulled out with a satin ribbon:
a teaspoon, a baby carriage.

Tell me why everyone who stood with me in a circle in that city
around that cake has left.

*

If she could find it, the artist marked the back of each drawer, the buckled
wood, with an inscription, where each drawer was found.

*

After my reading, the student raised his hand and asked: What can your
poetry do for New Orleans? What do you hope will happen if you write
about the hurricane?

*

The drawers make a wall but keep out nothing.

*

Where is the viewing area? It is everywhere.

Compendium of Lost Objects

Not the butterfly wing, the semiprecious stones,
      the shard of mirror,

not the cabinet of curiosities built with secret drawers
      to reveal and conceal its contents,

but the batture, the rope swing, the rusted barge
      sunk at the water's edge

or the park's Live Oaks you walked through
      with the forbidden man

or the pink-shuttered house on the streetcar line
      where you were married

or the green shock of land off I-10, road leading
      you away from home.

Not any of this
but a cot at the Superdome sunk in a dumpster

and lace valances from a Lakeview kitchen where water
      rose six feet high inside

and a refrigerator wrapped in duct tape lying
      in the dirt of a once-yard

and a Blue Roof and a house marked O and a

kitchen clock stopped at the time the hurricane hit.

Because, look, none of this fits
in a dark wood cabinet for safekeeping.

This is an installation
      for dismantling
            —never seen again.

NOTES

"Breach"—This poem is indebted to Amy Newman's book *Fall* (Middletown, CT: Wesleyan University Press, 2004).

"Evacuation"—Text is taken from www.nola.com, www.jeffparish.net (comments by Aaron Broussard, Jefferson Parish president), and the Coast Guard's Web site, www .uscg.mil.

"Levee, from the French *To Raise*"—On April 29, 1927, the levee at Caernarvon, Louisiana, was dynamited, flooding Plaquemines Parish and St. Bernard Parish. It was allegedly done to keep New Orleans from flooding, but the action targeted poor African Americans in the lower parishes while preserving the homes of people in greater New Orleans. See John Barry, *The Great Mississippi Flood and How It Changed America* (New York: Simon & Schuster, 1997).

"Four Studies of the Afterlife"—The four photographs referenced here were taken by photographer Chris Jordan and appear in his book *In Katrina's Wake: Portraits of Loss from an Unnatural Disaster* (New York: Princeton Architectural Press, 2006).

"Dear City"—All quotations from www.cnn.com, September 2005.

"Death of an American City"—Italicized text in this poem is from an editorial titled "Death of an American City," in the *New York Times*, December 11, 2005.

"The Superdome: A Suite"—This poem was inspired by Spike Lee's documentary film about Hurricane Katrina, *When the Levees Broke*.

"Divert the River"—This poem borrows language from Cornelia Dean's article "Time to Move the Mississippi, Experts Say," in the *New York Times*, September 19, 2006.

"Storyland"—This poem invokes Jim Amos's piece "Do Not Forsake Us," in the *Washington Post*, November 27, 2005, where he suggests that New Orleans after Katrina is "two cities."

"Disaster, A Poetics"—This poem was sparked by Jana Napoli's installation piece *Floodwall*, which was composed of drawers she collected after the hurricane in New Orleans and exhibited at the Liberty Street Bridge, New York City, January 2007.